PROPA PROPAGANDA

Benjamin Zephaniah

PROPA PROPAGANDA

BLOODAXE BOOKS

Copyright © Benjamin Zephaniah 1996

ISBN: 978 1 85224 372 2

First published 1996 by
Bloodaxe Books Ltd,
Eastburn,
South Park,
Hexham,
Northumberland NE46 1BS.

www.bloodaxebooks.com
For further information about Bloodaxe titles
please visit our website or write to
the above address for a catalogue.

Supported using public funding by
ARTS COUNCIL
ENGLAND

Digital reprint of the 1996 Bloodaxe Books edition.

Dedicated to the memory of old Labour

VICTORY TO THE UNEMPLOYED

Acknowledgements

'To Be Seen, To Be Done' first appeared in a book called *Out of the Night* published by New Clarion Press. The book is a collection of writings from prisoners on Death Row but as an editor of the book I was asked to submit a poem. It is one of the most powerful books of poetry and essays I've ever read and I am very proud to have played my part in it.

'The War Process' first appeared in *An Idea for Bosnia*, published jointly by Autumn House and Feed the Children in 1995. I lived for a short while in the former Yugoslavia. It's the only place where I've ever had a number one in the pop charts; it really hurt to see a place I loved so much disintegrate so quickly.

'De Rong Song' and 'Walking Black Home' both appear in the book *Funky Chickens* (Penguin Books, 1996). The reason why some poems appear in both my adults and children's collections is because both groups seem to appreciate them in performance. I also believe that these are good examples of poems that transcend age groups.

The majority of these poems have been performed on television, radio, in concert and even in cyberspace at some time. It would be ridiculous to try and name them all.

A musical version of 'Dry' is on the album *Back to Roots* set free by Acid Jazz Records in 1995.

'Belly of de Beast' can be heard on the album *Belly of de Beast* released by the Ariwa record label in 1996.

'Want to be a Soldier' is on the album *Us an Dem* released by Island Records in 1990 and 'The Curse of Count Empire' appears as simply 'Empire' on the Bomb the Bass album *Clear*, another Island Record release in 1995.

The photo on the back cover was taken by a nice guy called Steve Hall. The photo on the front cover with me looking moody in the background was taken by Adrian Boot. Unfortunately I cannot trace the person who took the photo in the foreground that has me prophesying the downfall of Babylon, I have tried. If he does read this he should get in touch so that I can tell him how much he has changed my life. I would also like to thank Joseph Stalin for the use of his jacket.

https://benjaminzephaniah.com/

Contents

I Have a Scheme

I am here today my friends to tell you there is hope
As high as that mountain may seem
I must tell you
I have a dream
And my friends
There is a tunnel at the end of the light.
And beyond that tunnel I see a future
I see a time
When angry white men
Will sit down with angry black women
And talk about the weather,
Black employers will display notice-boards proclaiming,
'Me nu care wea yu come from yu know
So long as yu can do a good day's work, dat cool wid me.'

I see a time
When words like affirmative action
Will have sexual connotations
And black people all over this blessed country of ours
Will play golf,
Yes my friends that time is coming
And in that time
Afro-Caribbean and Asian youth
Will spend big money on English takeaways
And all police officers will be armed
With a dumplin,
I see a time
A time when the President of the United States of America
          will stand up and say,
'I inhaled
And it did kinda nice
So rewind and cum again.'
Immigration officers will just check that you are all right
And all black people will speak Welsh.

I may not get there my friends
But I have seen that time
I see thousands of muscular black men on Hampstead Heath
        walking their poodles
And hundreds of black female Formula 1 drivers
Racing around Birmingham in pursuit of a truly British
        way of life.
I have a dream
That one day from all the churches of this land we will hear
        the sound of that great old English spiritual,
Here we go, Here we go, Here we go.
One day all great songs will be made that way.

I am here today my friends to tell you
That the time is coming
When all people, regardless of colour or class, will have
        at least one Barry Manilow record
And vending-machines throughout the continent of Europe
Will flow with sour sap and sugarcane juice,
For it is written in the great book of multiculturalism
That the curry will blend with the shepherd's pie
        and the Afro hairstyle will return.

Let me hear you say
Multiculture
Amen
Let me hear you say
Roti, Roti
A women.

The time is coming
I may not get there with you
But I have seen that time,
And as an Equal Opportunities poet
It pleases me
To give you this opportunity
To share my vision of hope
And I just hope you can cope
With a future as black as this.

The Death of Joy Gardner

They put a leather belt around her
13 feet of tape and bound her
Handcuffs to secure her
And only God knows what else,
She's illegal, so deport her
Said the Empire that brought her
She died,
Nobody killed her
And she never killed herself.
It is our job to make her
Return to Jamaica
Said the Alien Deporters
Who deport people like me
It was said she had a warning
That the officers were calling
On that deadly July morning
As her young son watched TV.

An officer unplugged the phone
Mother and child were now alone
When all they wanted was a home
A child watch Mummy die,
No matter what the law may say
A mother should not die this way
Let human rights come into play
And to everyone apply.
I know not of a perfect race
I know not of a perfect place
I know this is not a simple case
Of Yardies on the move,
We must talk some Race Relations
With the folks from immigration
About this kind of deportation
If things are to improve.

Let it go down in history
The word is that officially
She died democratically
In 13 feet of tape,
That Christian was over here
Because pirates were over there
The Bible sent us everywhere
To make Great Britain great.
Here lies the extradition squad
And we should all now pray to God
That as they go about their job
They make not one mistake,
For I fear as I walk the streets
That one day I just may meet
Officials who may tie my feet
And how would I escape.

I see my people demonstrating
And educated folks debating
The way they're separating
The elder from the youth,
When all they are demanding
Is a little overstanding
They too have family planning
Now their children want the truth.
As I move around I am eyeing
So many poets crying
And so many poets trying
To articulate the grief,
I cannot help but wonder
How the alien deporters
(As they said to press reporters)
Can feel absolute relief.

Terrible World

I've seen streets of blood
Redda dan red
There waz no luv
Just bodies dead
And I think to myself
What a terrible world.

I've seen pimps and priests
Well interfused
Denying peace
To the kids they abuse
And I think to myself
What a terrible world.

The killer who's the hero
The rapist who's indoors
The trade in human cargo
And dead poets on tours
I've seen friends put in jail
For not being rich
And mass graves made
From a football pitch.

I've seen babies scream
Nobody cared
Civilians starve
Whilst troops are prepared
And I think to myself
What a terrible world
Yes I think to myself
What a terrible world.

I do love Louis Armstrong's work but I thought I should walk
the same road and see things from a different point of view.

White Comedy

I waz whitemailed
By a white witch,
Wid white magic
An white lies,
Branded a white sheep
I slaved as a whitesmith
Near a white spot
Where I suffered whitewater fever.
Whitelisted as a white leg
I waz in de white book
As a master of de white art,
It waz like white death.

People called me white jack
Some hailed me as white wog,
So I joined de white watch
Trained as a white guard
Lived off de white economy.
Caught an beaten by de whiteshirts
I waz condemned to a white mass.

Don't worry,
I shall be writing to de Black House.

Belly of de Beast

Don't want go a jail, Don't want go a jail
Cause everytime me gu dea, dem never give me bail

In hell places like dat
Yu find no justice fe de Blacks
One time dem beat me almost kill me
An dem abuse me locks,
De Social Worker tell me
Bout me rights to a phone
But when de devils got me number
Devils raided me mudder's home.

Don't want go a jail, Don't want go a jail
Cause everytime me gu dea, dem never give me bail

Dem stop me jogging one fine day
As I got healthy on de green,
De Officer waz saying tings dat I would call obscene,
Once more I am in de van
Wid a beating to de station
Dat is what dem call helping investigations.

Dis is not de Jail House Rock
Dis is not de Jail House Rock
Yes dis is not

When dying in jail
You get pure unfit food fe eat
An Rasta minded vegan humans
Never get a treat,
Dem pack de place wid Blacks
There's a lack of common sense
An most Black people in dea
Is very innocent,

I think some politician man ....Should gu a jail
Some policeman ....Should gu a jail
Some slave driver ....Should gu a jail
An Margaret Thatcher (in my humble opinion) ..Should gu a jail

In state-owned homes like dat
Dere is no justice fe de Whites
In weird places like dat
Dem juss ignore yu human rights,
It really kinda lonely
An yu never get no peace
Dat is what de Rastas call
De belly of de beast.

Don't want go a jail, Don't want go a jail
Cause everytime me gu dea, dem never give me bail

Tax inspectors ....May like a stay in jail
Big city hustlers ....May like a stay in jail
Gun manufacturers ....May like a stay in jail
An de one John Major (it is alleged) ....May like a stay in jail

Dis is not de Jail House Rock
Dis is not de answer
Elvis
Dis is not.

De Rong Song

Your house is
Falling down
Around
Your
Feet,
And you got
Nought
To eat,
Don't worry
Be happy.

Your fish
Have drowned
You wear
A frown,
You search
But you don't
Own a pound,
Don't worry
Be happy.

You ain't got
Nowhere to
Play,
Just balconies
And
Motorways,
Don't worry
Be happy.

You meet
Someone
You really like,
They tell you to
Get on your bike
Don't worry
Be happy.

You're on your bike
And all is fine,
You get caught
In a washing line,
Don't worry
Be happy.

You go to school
The school is
Gone,
The Government
Put pressure on,
Don't worry
Be happy.

Your tea is
Dry
Your ice is
Hot,
Your head is
Tied up in a
Not,
Don't worry
Be happy.

You worry
Because
You're hurrying,
And hurry
Because
You're worrying,
Don't happy
Be worried.

Save Our Sons (SOS)

We black men of England
Too proud to cry for shame,
Let's cry a sea
Cry publicly,
Expose our very pain,
For Babylon the bandit
Is on our sisters' trail,
The bad talk
And the cool walk
Will not keep us out of jail.

We black men of England
Our guns are killing us,
How dare we?
Now hear me
How great is dangerous?
There's a fascist and a druggist
Out to get our kith and kin,
Let silent guns
Save our sons
The power is within.

We black men of England
Excel as if in sport
For our people,
Because some people
Want to see our face in court,
When we black men of England
Look the mirror in the face,
Through our sisters' eyes
We men shall rise
As proud sons of our race.

Reggae Head

Doctors inject me
Police arrest me
Dem electric shock me
But dat nar stop me,
Oooh
Dem can't get de Reggae out me head.

Dem tek me to a station
Put me pon probation,
But I still a dance
Wid de original nation,
Oooh
Dem can't get de Reggae out me head.

Dem sey,
Obey yu masta
Stop talk Rasta,
But I tek a dub
An juss rock a little fasta,
Noooo
Dem can't get de Reggae out me head.

Dem sey
Bad bowy, stop it,
Dem put money in me pocket
Riddim wise I drop it
An rock it Reggaematic,
Got it
Dem can't get de Reggae out me head.

Dem put
Pill an potions ina me
Dem put
Sum weird notion ina me,

Dem put
Fire water ina me
Wan time dem try fe slaughter me,
But I thrive on electricity
Dem tings stimulate I mentally
Now dem calling me de enemy
Cause de reggae roots deep ina me.
Experts debate me
Pop charts
Hate me,
De BNP want to
Annihilate me,
Oooh
Dem can't get de Reggae out me head.

Critics curse
Psychiatrists wail,
Cadburys
Lock me up in jail,
Still
Dem can't get de Reggae out me head.

Computers study me
Commuters worry me
But dem can't hurry me
Or do me injury,
No
Dem can't get de Reggae out me head.

Videos are watching me
But dat is not stopping me
Let dem cum wid dem authority
An dem science and technology,
But
Dem can't get de Reggae out me head.

Dry

Valley deep
Mountain high
Path so steep
Body dry,
Give me
Water.
Thousands of miles
Thousands of years
I come thru
To get I here,
Give me
Water.

I survived de ship
De governor's trick
Nu need to panic
I am dealing wid it,
Juss give me
Water.
Not juss me
Me people a cum
Wid Marcus Garvey
An dey all need sum,
Give dem
Water.

Me nar chat slackness
Or do malpractice,
I have nu weapon
To pose like a war man,
I need
Peace man
Love man
An
Lubrication,
Juss give me
Water.

Meditate and Communicate

A Sadhu
Like a lotus
Sits on India,
Waiting for the truth
To take him home,
And India
Is busy
Getting busier,
Trying to repay its World Bank Loan.

The Sadhu
Takes his ganja
Like a Rastaman,
He blesses it
And burns it
For the nation,
And as the smoke arrives
In central Pakistan,
The Sadhu talks to God
In meditation.

One day
They say
Gods will return to India,
And all our mixed up lives
Will fall in place,
But first the Gods
Must deal with Bombay's Mafia,
And the Mafia
Control a lot of space.

A Sadhu
Like a lotus
Sits on India,
Waiting for the truth
To take him home,
He's a pure
And dedicated
Meditator,
He's just meditating
With his mobile phone.

India 1993

More Animal Writes

They got death machines
And crooked cops,
They grin and scheme
And fire shots,
They have the power
We have not,
Animals must stick together.

They got Criminal Injustice Acts
And old grey men
Ignoring facts,
Cups full of evil
To the max,
Animals must stick together.

I saw murder on their plates
I could not count the murder rate,
I watched them celebrate the hate,
Animals must stick together.

They ate a penis
And a lung,
They drank the piss
And ate the tongue,
Each one of them
Was highly strung,
Animals must stick together.

The market force was powerful
The force got international,
They could not see their animal
They just could not get spiritual,
They had to hide to do their deeds
But every animal has needs,
As they drank the blood of greed
They failed to overstand the weed.

So animals put courage on
Picket,
Protest,
Let them be gone,
Us animals should stand as one,
Animals should stick together.
Do what Jill wants us to do
See the animal in you,
Let us not stop
Until we've got
A world that Jill
Would like a lot,
And to do that
United act,
Animals must stick together.

Dedicated to Jill Phipps who died under the wheel of a truck whilst
demonstrating against live animal exports at Coventry in 1995.

Who Dun It?

Soldiers unite
De war is over
Now people hav fe talk
An get fe know each other
Exiles flying home like birds going south
Because Mandela is in an apartheid is out,
Day dream a multiracial dream
Day see de grim reality
Recall dat hand dat waz unseen
Before de peoples victory,
Dere is much work dat must be done
No sense in living in de past
Still dere's smoke comin from de gun
So there are questions I muss ask
But,
Nobody done apartheid
Day were all revolutionaries.

Nobody took de land an divided de people
Dere waz no reason to build townships
Cause nobody done no evil,
Nobody introduce a state of emergency
Nobody did anything so no one is guilty,
Nobody banned de books
No one set up road blocks
Everybody waz supporting de Communists an Blacks
Everybody knew apartheid put in practice would not work
Yes, everybody waz protecting de Blacks from getting hurt,
Yes,
Nobody done apartheid
Day were all revolutionaries.

Dere were no
Black hotels　　White hotels
Black music　　White music
An if dere waz, all hated it
An everyone waz fighting it,

No
Black parks　　White parks
Black trains　　White trains
Black land　　White land
An other land fe Indians

Nobody killed Steve Biko
No
Dere were no Pass Laws
Day were all at Soweto
Fighting fe de cause,
Nobody watch Sophiatown burn
No ting waz in de banks
Nobody haz a lesson to learn
No one voted in de tanks,
Dat's right,
Nobody done apartheid
Day were all revolutionaries.
So no one wants revenge
An dere's no one to avenge
De boycotts an de protests were not needed,
All muss now pretend dere's no past
An become friends
An juss sey tings like
Common sense succeeded.

Now a moments silence
For dem dat could not stay,

An a moment of nonviolence
For dem dat passed away,

Yet more moments to remember
De times yu muss forget
Why go to Australia?
Dere's nothing to regret
Because,
Nobody done apartheid
Day were all revolutionaries.

I'd juss like fe know
How a hater thought
An how it waz to play around
At segregated sport,
I'd juss like fe know
How day will cope wid words like
Share,
An how it waz day slept at night
When death waz everywhere,
I'd juss like fe know
What made dem tick an tock
An what's it like to be on top
Den find yu hav to stop,
I'd juss like fe know
What day think of those next door
An if day still believe de land is theirs
For evermore,
But,
Nobody done apartheid
Day were all revolutionaries.

South Africa 1995

The Angry Black Poet

Next on stage
We have the angry black poet,
So angry
He won't allow himself to fall in luv,
So militant
You will want to see him again.
Don't get me wrong
He means it,
He means it so much
He is unable to feel,
He's so serious
If he is found smiling
He stops to get serious before he enters stage left,
Through days he dreams of freedom
Through nights he rants of freedom,
Tonight he will speak for you,
Give him a hand.

Please give him a hand,
Help him,
He too has silent moments
He could do without,
I have worked with him
And I know
He needs stroking
He needs to play
Let him know you are there.

I knew him when he was unknown
I knew him when he was happy,
Now he's angry
You will luv him,
He lives on the edge
He has highs and lows,

And I know
He hates publicity
And he luvs you all,
Be quiet
And let's hear it for
The angry black poet.

Poor Millionaires

I heard a man singing
De millionaire blues,
Him sey
'Me can't tek it,
Too much pressure.'

I heard a man singing
De blues of fame,
Him sey
'Reggae is
Wonderful blues.'

I heard a man singing
Jamaican blues,
Him sey
'Rap dat bad bass line
Wid luv.'

I heard a man singing
Millionaire blues,
With his militant
Peace luving band,
I heard a man singing
Millionaire blues,
As he basically
Lived off de land.

Written in Memphis, Tennessee and first published there
by River City Press.

Silence in Our Screams

People demonstrating
Fe de right to silence,
And fe right to do dat
Wid no violence.
We will chant
Fe de right to silence
Sing fe de right to silence
Shout fe de right to silence
An die fe it.

We shall not be moved
Until free to wander round.
Relax don't panic
We are nomadic,
Not far off ones on TV
Just call us your family,
We are in our own backyard
We and foxes find it hard.

When they should consider
Miscarriages of justice,
In come de criminal justice kill.
Can't see no justice,
Just us
An dem,
We're going backwards my friend.

De dreadlocked
Travelling poet
Is shouting fe de right to silence.
For crying out loud
Monks are crying out loud
Fe de right to silence,
De most peaceful people in de land
Fighting fe de right to silence,

Librarians an singers
Want de right to silence,
Nature said we should
Learn to luv silence.

So we're going back to SUS
We're back to basic rules,
Our memories are long
Two wrongs are simply wrong,
So the state will make a fuss
When de workers down their tools
All of dis an still no rights
To silence.

Silence
Shout it,
Silence.
Shout it,
Bang your drum
For precious

Silence.

This poem was written for the pressure group Liberty as a sister poem to
Adrian Mitchell's 'Criminal Justice for Crying Out Loud – A Rant'. (He
likes short, snappy titles.) It was to be used in Liberty's campaign against
the Criminal Justice Act, I don't know if it was ever used but Adrian and I
felt we had to respond in our own way anyway and I like to think of this
piece as the result of passionate, poetic intercourse.

Back to What

Back to basics
Back to the cave
Back to the Ice Age
Back to what

Back to basics
Back to the plague
Back to the Stone Age
Back to what

Back to basics
Back on your knees
Back with diseases
Back to what

Back to basics
Back to the sleaze
Back if you please
Back to what

Back to basics
Back to the creator
Back to Africa
Back to what

Back to basics
Back to back
Back to Black
Back to what.

A copy of this poem has been sent to John Major.

To Be Seen, To Be Done

If you are to be seen
Why hide
Behind curtains, robes
Order and law,
If you are so true
Why lie
To the mouths that speak
Of you,
Why bite
The hand
That's feeding you.

If you are to live with us
Why not
Protect us,
We need you now
And always,
For ever
And ever
Be good,
If you want respect
Just be
As equal as we,
What do you mean
Without we.

You came to save our madness
But madness turned you on,
We have one question
Justice,
That is,
Where have you gone??

One Day in Babylon

I met someone called loneliness
Who wanted me to stay
Because I told him I need friends
He would not go away,
I slept with mad and sadness
They wrapped me in their arms
The orgasms were full of woe
The poisons full of charm.
I spent one moon in fucking hell
My Black was bought and sold
In there I saw the White slave driver
Quickly growing old,
I met the foolish High Priest
Who told me what to be
I watch the foolish die hard die
Full of iniquity.
I met my ego long ago
It covered me in shame
I killed that cancer killing me
I found joy in its pain,
I saw my anger mocking me
I cried as I admired
And I saw great hypocrisy
Looking very tired.

City Lights

Screaming children,
Battered children,
Citizens advice,
Outside
Is a Rolls Royce,
With
People who look nice,
Down in my city.

Newspaper lies,
Government spies,
Another purse robbed,
A woman sits and sobs,
It happens without pity
Down in my city.

Bored teenagers beating strangers
In some dark alley,
They tried it once with me
Down in my city...

This is one of the first poems I ever wrote down, it was also the
inspiration behind the title of my last Bloodaxe book *City Psalms*
but then silly me forgot to include it in the collection.

No Problem

I am not de problem
But I bare de brunt
Of silly playground taunts
An racist stunts,
I am not de problem
I am a born academic
But dey got me on de run
Now I am branded athletic,
I am not de problem
If yu give I a chance
I can teach yu of Timbuktu
I can do more dan dance,
I am not de problem
I greet yu wid a smile
Yu put me in a pigeon hole
But I am versatile.

These conditions may affect me
As I get older,
An I am positively sure
I hav no chips on me shoulders,
Black is not de problem
Mother country get it right,
An juss fe de record,
Sum of me best friends are white.

Family Values

Reds are in yu beds
Banks are in de red
Bombs in de city
Taxes burn
Crime rates soar
Hospitals fight
Schools rebel
Water kills
Cops kill,
Cover-ups uncovered
Neo-nazis rise
Pension funds not trusted
Talks fail
War looms
An yu hav de cheek to call me
A
Problem
Child.

Dancing the Tradition

No people nu cry
No Jah people nu cry,
Cause I remember yu just today
Swinging an swaying
To dat music   saying
So much trouble in de world.

Yes people nu cry
De rebel nu die,
Cause I remember
How just today we sat
Ina government yard in Handsworth,
An when de Babylon cum
We nu run,
We went in concert   singing,
Get up, stand up
Stand up for your rights.

When I see yu yesterday
Dancing yu movement of Exodus,
I tell yu Bob Marley lives,
An den agen yu an yu fren
Continually skanking like dere is no end,
I repeat, Bob Marley lives.

Hey people, we talkin Conquering Lion of Jamaica here,
We talkin de buffalo soldier,
Yu sing song sang along
Wid de dread dat shot de sheriff
After yu chased de crazy baldhead minds,
So where's de death in dat?

Don't cry,
Feel no pain
Cause de people will not wait in vain
Dying to go to heaven ina Jesus name,
An if yu can still dig de
Singer writer poet prophet,
Don't cry, Rock it!
Duz dat feel ded to you.

Forward,
Let us be iron
Like de lion from Zion,
We who walk wid de lion within,
We who harmonise wid de lion
Should know better.
Se no people nu cry,
Trenchtown Jamaica has gone outernational
An St Anns has lifted her hands towards de heavens,
Smile Jamaica,
De world is listening.

In de abundance of water
De fool is thirsty,
Let us drink,
Herb wine
Honey strong drink
Let us think,
Where de hell did we get
Dis simple idea of death?

Neighbours

I am the type you are supposed to fear
Black and foreign
Big and dreadlocks
An uneducated grass eater.

I talk in tongues
I chant at night
I appear anywhere,
I sleep with lions
And when the moon gets me
I am a Wailer.

I am moving in
Next door to you
So you can get to know me,
You will see my shadow
In the bathroom window,
My aromas will occupy
Your space,
Our ball will be in your court.
How will you feel?

You should feel good
You have been chosen.

I am the type you are supposed to love
Dark and mysterious
Tall and natural
Thinking, tea total.
I talk in schools
I sing on TV
I am in the papers,
I keep cool cats

And when the sun is shining
I go Carnival.

Another World

Those ships trespassed on my religion
Those hands strangled my life,
Those diseases infected my grass,
Dear teacher,
          I have a problem with Columbus.

Dat sperm put blue in my black
For once I became Capitalism,
You can call it America,
Canada
Or Rhodesia,
I call it Ours,
You can call it free
Democratic
Or the state of something,
I call it Earth.

We went to visit him
We did not steal from him,
We told him Anansi stories
We played Kabaddi with him.
He came to us,
He done physical and spiritual burglary
He shared the loot with his family,
My family was devastated.
Dear teacher,
          I am not into Columbus.

Dear teacher,
          Do you know what we are going through?
Have been through,
Or where we have been,
Our wise ones have been assassinated,
Our social services
Are in museums.

Ever heard of the Nubians?
Nubians are we,
Is the price right?
Priceless are we.
We are thirteen months a year
Not cargo,
We are past, present and future
Not His Story,
Look teacher,
           I have a problem with Columbus.

There is a younger version of this poem called 'Civil Lies' in my book
Talking Turkeys published by Penguin Children's Books.

The War Process

Cease-fire planned	Cease-fire coming
Talks planned	Peace broker coming
Talks postponed.	Cease-fire broken.
Mediators in place	Deadline imposed
Tuff negotiations	Tension grows
Negotiations breakdown.	Deadline goes.
Cease-fire planned	UN repeats
Talks on talks talked	UN repeats
Airport taken.	UN repeats.
UN debates	Mediators in place
Resolutions made	Foothill taken
Deadline imposed.	Talks breakdown.
Deadline coming	UN debates
Reinforcements coming	Factions debate
Deadline gone.	Factions don't budge.
Massacre discovered	Cease-fire planned
Cover up uncovered	Cease-fires come
Hard line taken.	Cease-fires go.

Refugees talk.

My Rwandan friend said,
'At least they have ceasefires in Bosnia.'

My Bosnian friend said,
'What is a ceasefire,
By the way?'

Want To Be a Soldier

De life of a soldier is very hard
Dem never wid dem families dem always is abroad
It teks a tough guy to live on de edge
It teks courage to mek de pledge,
It teks yu independence an yu sanity
Yu muss hav strong feelings fe yu flag an country
De church will bless de killings but yu muss do de deed
De man up in de office will give yu all dat yu need,
De life of a soldier is physical
Wars hav laws so yu can kill an look respectable
De life of a soldier is demanding
It teks hard eyes to witness suffering.

So yu want to be a soldier
Well are yu tough enough?
An are yu young an strong
An flowing wid de right stuff
So yu want to be a soldier
Do yu need an enemy or is it juss de wages
Do yu need security to kill?

De road from machoism leads to masochism
A young man like yuself could always earn a living killing,
Never shed a tear when yu see de sight of blood
Do what yu are ordered never do a thing fe love,
Yu don't need to know what's right
An dere's a chance yu'll be de victor
De lads in de regiment will put yu in de picture,
Yu might not live fe long but yu could die glorious
It is a risky business but yu're doing it fe us
Yes yu're doing it fe us an future generations
It haz something to do wid international relations
Yu've seen de commercials, yu've taken in de hype
An yu hav reason to believe yu are de right type.

So yu want to be a soldier
Well are yu tough enough.

Now look at dat,
Juss look at dat
Yu're gunning yu neighbour
But yu hav an excuse fe dis very bad behaviour
Yu're pointing to de Bible, yu're blaming history
Now yu hav left half of de world in bloody misery.

Yu may want to play a soldier
I want to play at getting older.

Sit Con

Cover our wounds
With Black Comedies,
Laugh
At our expense.

Cover our wounds
With your cause,
Claim our
Olympic golds.

Cover our sexuality
With religion,
And give
God blue eyes.

Cover our rain dance
With discos,
Get down
To the beats you despise.

Hide our stones
In your crown jewels,
What goes
Must come,
We wait.

Hide our beauty
In your views,
So the rich Black
Buys a nose.

Cover our liberty monuments
With a ballot
And a referendum.

Cover our wounds
With Black Comedies,
And keep smiling
When we get our freedom.

City River Blues

Went to the river
Seeking inspiration,
Saw dead fish floating
Dead men boating
And condoms galore.

Sat by the river
Wondering,
From where cometh
Dat bloody smell,
For if I waz wize
And I could tell
The world would know.

This is our river
It runs through our lives
This is our river
Our shit-coloured river,
It's had it
But it's ours.

This river speaks
Every boot had a body
Every shirt had a friend,
And the old boys
Say they shall all meet
Where every river ends.

Here by this river
Joe Public wrote songs
And ships came
From far away,
Capitalism lived here,
Ships left from here,
To cheat someone,
Somewhere.

This river is on the map
The Queen came here,
The King came here,
Hitler bombed it,
Joe Bloggs bombed it,
A hundred factories
Bomb it every day,
But this river won't go away,
They say.

Went to the river
Seeking inspiration,
Got eco-depression,
Got stopped and searched,
Got called a coon,
Got damned lungs,
Got city river blues.

Tricky

When I grow up I want to be a student,
With God's help I could become Darwinian,
But my mother wants me to be jurisprudent,
And my wife wants me to be a lesbian.

Altered Ego

A small geezer called Wacko Jacko
Waz trying his best to act macho
He moved just a bit
An his trousers split
An out popped a sixties style afro.

Homeward Bound

That old man
Cut sugarcane in Jamaica
After he graduated from Sunday School,
Fed up with cutting cane
He came here for a better life.
He came here on a big ship
With big dreams
And two guineas,
He came here full of hope
With a great big smile,
He came here for the welcome
And the promise.
If his mother (bless her soul) could see him now
She would cry for her baby.

He don't understand political correctness
Give him the money and he's gone,
He did not study the oral tradition
Give him a stage and
He will explain.
He came here with his ambitions
And his Christianity,
She came here with a nursery qualification
And his Christianity,
Between them they produced six Rastafarians
Who called themselves Lost Africans.

When the old man puts on his old suit
He dances like a rude boy
His music is in his head,
Now he dreams of fresh sugar cane,
When the old man
Puts on his everyday face
He is only grinning and bearing,
He did forty years on the buses
And he never went to jail.

That old man
Was going home anyway,
All his Jamaica nights are in his head,
Fed up with the weather
He wants a better life,
All his English days he voted Labour
But he thinks that Labour didn't vote for him,
And now he only wants to see his saviour
Sweet Jamaica.

That old man
Shall die in Kensal Rise
He knows it,
You know it
But don't tell him.

Parents Today

The problem with children today
Is their parents,
The problem with their parents
Was their parents,
And their parents had big problems
With their parents.

Parents lead children astray
So parents should pay,
Where are the parents
That taught innocent children
Smart bomb creation,
Who taught children how to succeed
In the Slave Trade,
Who on earth taught lost explorers
How to discover ancient civilisations.

Whose parents dare to
Send other parents
To war
Creating
Single
Parents?
Where are the parents?

Parents were sitting at home
Whilst parents burnt the city,
Parents were sent to stop parents
Burn the city,
Parents preach that parents are the problem
And parents told the preacher he was wrong,
And now that parents are on the agenda,
Parents are after the parents vote
And they will get it
One way or the other.

The Curse of Count Empire

I am looking at your soul
As you're selling it out
I am looking at you straight
As you mess me about,
I am looking at your future
I am looking at your past
I am looking at you looking at me
Through the looking glass,
As I look into your eye
I see another lie,
I look into your closet
And I see another spy,
I wonder why you are not
Looking at you,
Because you gotta know yourself.

You gotta feel yourself
And let go
You gotta know you reap
What you sow,
You gotta feel something
At some time,
Check the writings on the wall
And look into the sign,
You're spending all your money
On games that never work,
You're wasting all your energy
And everywhere it hurts,
God it really hurts
Yes it really hurts,
You gotta know yourself.

If you spit in de sky
It could fall in your eye
You see what goes up comes down

You will die looking out
If you're not looking in
You just gotta know yourself.

I am looking at your pastures
And they were never green,
I am looking for your justice
And it cannot be seen,
I am checking where you're coming from
And where you're going to,
I am checking out what you have done
To see what you can do,
I am looking at your law books
And they were never red,
I am looking at your locks boy
And they cannot be dread,
I am looking at your empire
Slipping down the drain
Hey, you gotta know yourself.

My sister said you are a vampire
And you feed on the life of a pure heart
A metaphor for empire
You suck the life from goodness,
A kinda Dracula
Feeding on the life found in a pure heart
A half dead vampire
How you made bad the goodness.

Well empires come and empires go
Another lesson to be learnt
Another history to know,
Every tree is known by the fruit it bears
And I see no love anywhere you appear,
My sister calls you England
Dis is not the past
New England.

A re-write of a duet originally performed with Sinéad O'Connor
on the 'Bomb the Bass' album *Clear* (Island Records).

Art

Poems are read my love
Sad songs are blue
Love songs are sweet my love
And all great art is true.

Words

Thunder makes me thunder
Lightning makes me light
Poems make me wonder
About the words I write.

Hope

Folk like me think
Is there hope?
When folk like me
Are scared to vote.

Mad Human Disease

U - ME + £ + $
Often referred to as Blind Consumerism

An infectious mental disease caused by a virus which attacks
the soft tissues of the brain.
Characteristics of the condition have been known to transmit
from one generation to another with the rich and educated
being the most susceptible persons.
Mutations in the virus are frequent and the immunity usually
does not affect new, antigenically different strains.
Sufferers will do anything for money and early signs of the
condition are:

1) Working for a living and not really living.
2) Reading newspapers that don't make sense and believing
them.
3) Inflammation of the ego for no reason at all.
4) Voluntary twitching of facial muscles producing plastic smiles.
5) Progressive healthyfoodaphobia.
6) The feeding of brains and testicles to vegetarian cows.

Aggression is increased in immunocompromised persons and
a form of illusion known as 'the God complex' will occur.
It is not advisable to see your doctor concerning the condition
because most doctors are known sufferers.
Recommended treatment: a serious intake of common sense
which is now available without prescription.

CAUTION
A European ban is not a permanent cure.

Master, Master

Master master drank a toast
And dreamt of easy tea,
He gave to you a Holy Ghost,
    Come children see.

From Liverpool on sinking ships
Blessed by a monarchy,
To Africa the hypocrites,
    Come children see.

Master master worked the slave
Who ran for liberty,
The master made us perm and shave,
    Come children see.

If slave drivers be men of words
We curse that poetry,
Its roots you'll find are so absurd,
    Come children see.

Master master's sons drill oil
It's all his legacy,
They put the devil in the soil,
    Come children see.

Fear not his science or his gun
Just know what you can be,
And children we shall overcome,
    Come children see.

Tis true that we have not now chains
Yet we were never free,
Still master's chains corrupt our brains,
    Come children see.

A word is slave for man is man
What's done is slavery,
The evils of the clan that can,
    Come children see.

Master master worked the slave
The upright sort was he,
That boy dug master master's grave
    Come children see.

Some now await a judgement day
To know his penalty,
It's blood and fire anyway,
    Come children see.

Cybersex

I heard dat out in cyberspace
There is a very special place
Where you can go and have a taste
Of three-dimensional love.

When I heard dis I said all right
I have to taste this new delight
I had to find that love web site
For three-dimensional love.

I found a hacker jacking-in
With a friendly server serving him
I surf because I cannot swim
For three-dimensional love.

My modem waz performing fine
The clock said it was cybertime
All my emotions went on line
For three-dimensional love.

In virtual reality
The database waz dating me
I still kept my virginity
For three-dimensional love.

High without any narcotics
In search of some cyberotics
I search through all related topics
On three-dimensional love.

I found it, it was so attractive
Its interface was just perfective
And we got very interactive
On three-dimensional love.

I felt my mouse go wild and spasm
This is not no pleonasm
We blew a great big cyborgasm
Sweet three-dimensional love.

Ageism

I am an old scribe
From a long time,
With a restless mind
And Rastafari eyes.

I am the world you forget
(Or choose to erase),
The one you fear
In your sleep.

I am the memory
That you don't discuss,
Check my kind
I am your future.

I am your place of birth,
I am your good news,
Whose millennium are you?

I am not a star
Just a universe,
I am not just me
Still I am.

I am a way of life
With countless days,
I bring seasons
As I speak.

I am the I you debated
And I created
The hours before your time.

I am an old scribe,
From the first tribe,
Whose millennium are you?

Acts of Parliament: *motion 1*

Kissing de baby
Helping de poor
Helping old ladies
Giving us more,
Controlling inflation
Controlling the streets
Serving the nation
Denying defeats,
Dining with tyrants
Smiling on cue
Not liking violence
Caring for you,
Loving his woman
Loving her man
Being a human
And touring Japan,
Going to mosque
Going to church
Appearing on *Frost*
And doing research,
Wearing a poppy
Flying the flag
Supporting industry
Bombing Baghdad,
Visiting schools
And hospital wards
Observing rules
And more visits abroad,
The show just goes on
These are hard acts to follow
We're watching the con
It's on TV tomorrow.

Acts of Parliament: *motion 2*

John Major announced
Something.
Tony Blair said
Something.
Betty Boothroyd rose from her seat
And expounded
Something.
Something was debated
And something was agreed
And that was nothing.

Some times some things
Need
Changing.
Some things some times
Need something.
And politicians are
Something
Else.

The next time you see a politician
Tell them
Something.
And if you are visualistic
Show them
Something.
Today in Parliament
Something was made out of nothing
And nobody kept saying something.

Acts of Parliament: *motion 3*

Today in the House of the Lords
A busker waz strumming some chords,
When a Lord and Lady
Who both share a baby
Accompanied him with their snores.

The President Is Dead Again

for Ken Saro-Wiwa and his comrades

Believe me Mr President General
Some Africans want to die at home

These are not lazy men
These are men of words
The men your people luv
So now boss
Point your guns at your paymaster
And
Shoot,
Take your British arms and
Shoot
Your feet,
Watch your blood and the soil fraternise,
This soil is dead already.

Your corporate friends and city planners have died
Like the soil you killed
They be
Dead, dead, dead
How does it feel to be unburied
Or unincinerated?

President General and friends
Some Africans want to die at home
A natural death
With drummers and the tribe at hand.

A hummingbird tells me dat
Your jails are full of activists
Activists dat are full of life,
The vendor who sold you dat
Pretty, pretty, work of art
And the palace for its comfort

Cannot sell you the silence of the earth community
Or a silent history of your deeds,
Hence I see a day dead Mr President
When your very lovers shall look to earth
Asking
Why?
Look

Look
Check dis
We are watching you,
You do dark we see light
After all,
We are the world.

How many prisoners throats can you cut before you reach hell?
How many children can you stop from growing up?
And remember now
Your business friends will leave you
They will be
Gone,
Gone,
Gone,
Long before your financial returns.

De brothers on de streets who sey respect
Sey no respect
Because yu disrespect
And
A hummingbird tells me dat
Worms are eating you
Before you eat the worms,
You really need to be buried.

Why?
You a warrior wid a poxy mind
Why
Hang your doctor?

And when your death is so wordless
Why send your historians to Western capitals?
Listen, listen
Listen to me man
Run, run, run
Find a planet wid no Africa
And act White
De devil will luv you.

Believe me Mr President General
Some Africans want to die at home

Let me introduce you to the mothers

They run the universities
What future do you have for them?
Say now
Tell the BBC,
Then
Cry, cry, cry
All the way to the bank.

Mr President General you suck.
A burning spear is here
It came from within
To burn your serenity,
So sit on your throne
Godlike for now
Because you will not be celebrated
You suck presidentially
And the universe knows it.

How come you so educated
But you know not the size of Africa
You foolish sucker,
Your dream of being Mr Nigeria is foolish too
Listen,
Read,
Tek dis in,

Hell is no fun so
Breathe in
Burn yourself,
You will have no wages to pay
And no one will care,
Breathe in
Get your fire on the double,
Let me assure you that you will be
Remembered
For
Something.

Bad night Mr President
Don't have faith
Don't hope
And do not wish for forgiveness
Juss
Run, run, run
As slowly as you can

And
You may be buried soon,
All alone,
Your corporate friends will be like you
Elsewhere,
And
Those singers and those poets
Will
Appear.

Independence

No house
No money
No milk
No honey
But dis land is ours.

No bricks
No mortar
No private water,
No roads
No signs
No enemy mines,
No work
No play
Just dried up clay,
But what?
Dis land is ours.

That little piece of sun is ours
We borrow clouds from neighbours,
We got air
We got we
No industry
But we are free
And asking you no favours.

And who are you anyway?
What is your bank?

What is a gun?
What's meant by your rank?

Why do you have
That lust in your eyes?

Your holy book says
You're a typical lie.

No sweat
No pain
No MATERial gain,
But what?
Dis land is ours,
No wars to do
Dat's right
No you.

Sail on
Dis land is ours.

De Queen an I

It's nice to know dat de Queen
Sits at home studying me.
She study me history,
Wea me born
Me roots an fruits.
An when me go rave
De Queen an I are intellectually engaged.
She study me anatomy
She check out how me sexy,
She check me riddim an me rhyme
Me sleeping times,
I know she'll check dis
And she always check dat
She study me so much
Mek me proud to be Black.

Sometimes she will blow a fuse
When she get confuse by de news
Sometimes I know she want to talk to me
But de bodyguards will get jealous yu see,
So she treat me like a kinda
Open University
An study me casually.

Me Republican frens sey
If she study thee
Den study she,
But I done study she
Way back in 1983.
Frens sey
Examine her
But me check her out already
Now she studying Reggae,
I nar tell no lie
She a study Rastafari, guy.

Me is de Queen's book a bedtime
Her morning service
Her vital muse,
I don't know
Why it's so
I is just
De one she chose.
Me is her favourite lesson
Her liberation
Her poetry,
She don't like guys messin
I may be guessin
But I think dat's why she study me.

One is humble
One is honoured
One will never object
I am so happy
Dat she chose me
I am de Queen's subject.

Walking Black Home

That day waz
A bad day,

I walked for
Many miles,

Unlike me,
I did not

Return any
Smiles.

Tired,

Weak
And
Hungry,

But I
Would not
Turn

Back,

Sometimes it's hard
To get a taxi
When you're Black.

This one appears in my book *Funky Chickens* published
by Penguin Children's Books.

Self Defence

Rights fe Whites shout de BNP
An dem strategy is fe kill we,
We sey
We ago fight dem all de way,
Self defence is no offence
We will not simply run.

Ain't no Black in de Union Jack,
We stand an defend any attack,
Too many parents are crying
Because their children are dying,
And we can't get any protection
From a force wid racist connections,
As LKJ did say
We must stand and drive dem away,
Self defence is no offence
We will do what must be done.

It's a case of us and dem
Our lives we must defend
From de East End of London
To de Highlands of Scotland
We will fight dem to de end,
Self defence is no offence
We only have ourselves.

We only want peace but
Here comes de beast
Ignoring de truths and de facts,
Attacking de weak out on de streets
And we nar tolerate dat,
Self defence is no offence and
We can't wait fe no one else.

Tax Relief

Keep holding on it's cummin
Hang on
It's cummin soon,
Keep holding on it's cummin
Tax today
Jam tomorrow.

Now just hold on it's cummin
Soon cum
De day is soon,
Keep hold on it cummin
Tax today
Jam tomorrow.

Tomorrow will be cummin
Invest in jam today
Keep holding on it's cummin,
Jam tomorrow
Jam tomorrow
Jam tomorrow
Tax today.

Heckling Miss Lou

Kiss me neck
Dat one deh sweet,
Chat dat poem again Miss Lou,
Lard me God
Dat verse deh hard,
Run it wan more time.
Blouse an skirt bowy
What a rhyme,
Rewind an lyric again Miss Lou,
Jesus Christ
What good advice,
Cum wid a noddor line.

Whip I wid dat wicked word style
Move I wid yu riddim,
When yu done juss ress a while
Den start from de beginnin,
Teach me, touch me, test me,
Yu wordologist yu,
An when yu done unstress me
Poetically
Miss Lou.

Miss Lou (Louise Bennett) is the Queen of all we Dub, Reggae
or Performance Poets. To overstand the poetry of Jamaica or
its offspring you have to check out Miss Lou.

Childless

Strong biceps
Firm thighs,
Big bottom
Sexy eyes,
Fast
On the track,
Strong like
A lion,
Good Kung-fu feet
And healthy hair.

Strong triceps
No lie,
Rhymster
Nice guy,
A good healthy back
Great levels of iron,
There must be a baby
In there
Somewhere,
There must be
A baby
In here.